THE U.S. HOUSE OF REPRESENTATIVES

by Amy Kortuem

PEBBLE
a capstone imprint

Pebble Explore is published by Pebble, an imprint of Capstone.
1710 Roe Crest Drive
North Mankato, Minnesota 56003
www.capstonepub.com

Library of Congress Cataloging-in-Publication Data is available on the Library of Congress website.
ISBN 978-1-9771-1393-1 (hardcover)
ISBN 978-1-9771-1818-9 (paperback)
ISBN 978-1-9771-1402-0 (ebook pdf)

Summary: Describes how representatives are chosen, their duties, where they work, and more.

Image Credits

AP Images, 27; Newscom: Hill Street Studios Blend Images, Cover, Jeff Malet Photography, 10, 21, Polaris/Ron Sachs, 23, Reuters/Aaron Josefczyk, 9, Reuters/Brian Snyder, 13, Sipa USA/Alex Edelman - CNP, 25, Sipa USA/Ron Sachs, 18-19, UPI/Pat Benic, 20, VWPics/Terray Sylvester, 14, ZUMA Press/Bastiaan Slabbers, 15, ZUMA Press/Mark Rightmire, 17; Shutterstock: Alexkava, 6 (middle), america365, 6 (left, right), mark reinstein, 5, Orhan Cam, 24, Roman Babakin, 26

Design Elements

Shutterstock: ExpressVectors, In-Finity

Editorial Credits

Anna Butzer, editor; Cynthia Della-Rovere, designer;
Jo Miller, media researcher; Laura Manthe, production specialist

All internet sites appearing in back matter were available and accurate when this book was sent to press.

Printed and bound in China.
2489

Table of Contents

Words in **bold** are in the glossary.

What Is the House of Representatives?

There is a place where 435 people work for you. They listen to the people in the United States. They hear what the people want in the **government**. They help make **laws** the people want. This place is called the "people's house." It is the House of Representatives, or House.

The U.S. government has three branches, or parts. All of the branches work together. Each branch has a different job. They each have different rules to follow.

One of the branches is the **legislative branch**. This branch makes laws for our country. It has two parts, the House and the **Senate**. Together, the House and Senate make up the U.S. **Congress**.

U.S. Government

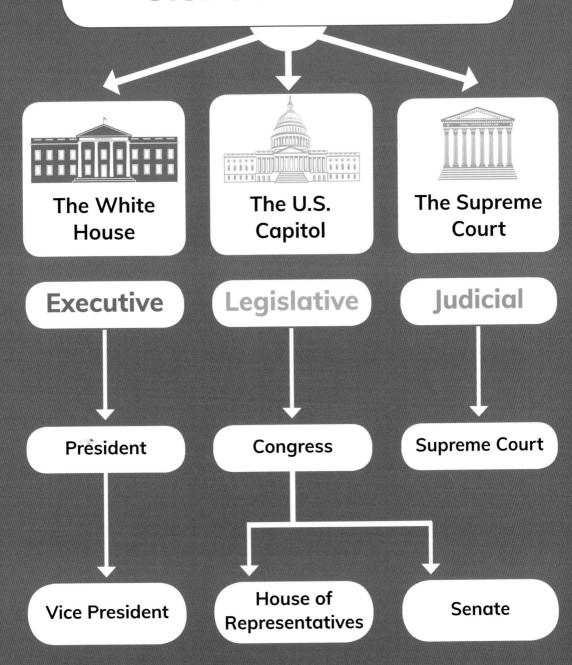

The White House	The U.S. Capitol	The Supreme Court
Executive	Legislative	Judicial
President	Congress	Supreme Court
Vice President	House of Representatives	Senate

Who Can Be a Representative?

Do you want to be a representative? There are rules about who can be one.

Representatives have to live in the United States for seven years. They need to live in the state they work for. They must be at least 25 years old.

Many representatives have other jobs as well. Some work as lawyers, business owners, or teachers.

Ohio representative Joyce Beatty

Each state has at least one member in the House. States with more people have more representatives. States with fewer people have less.

New representatives meet outside the U.S. Capitol in Washington, D.C.

For example, Rhode Island only has one member in the House. Other states, such as California, can have more than 50 members.

How Are Representatives Chosen?

People who want to be representatives must be part of an **election**. They travel around their states and listen to ideas from people. They learn about laws that people want or need. They talk to the people in their states. If the people like what they hear, they **vote** for the **candidates**.

A candidate speaks to people in his state.

Representatives have **terms** that are two years long. After two years, they must win another term. They can work in the House as long as they win terms. They can run for election as many times as they would like.

Pennsylvania representative
Brendan Boyle

What Do Representatives Do?

Representatives have many responsibilities. They meet with people and talk about ways to make the country better. They bring people's ideas to the House. They work with other members of Congress to make laws that people want and need.

A representative visits a school and talks with students.

What if there is a tie when we are voting for a president? The House of Representatives can choose the president.

Members choose between the three candidates with the most votes. Each state representative in the House gets one vote.

Representatives meet in a room called a chamber.

Each member of the House works in groups called **committees**. These groups meet and talk about ideas for new laws. Each group talks about different things. Some of these things include farming, education, and the environment.

The House has a leader called the Speaker. Members of the House choose the Speaker. The Speaker of the House leads meetings. The Speaker works with the Senate and the president to talk about **bills**.

The House passes bills, then they go to the Senate. Then the president either signs or **vetoes** them.

The Speaker of the House leads the House of Representatives.

Where Do Representatives Work?

Representatives meet in the Capitol building in Washington, D.C. They sit in a big room called the House Chamber. Seats face the Speaker of the House in front.

The room has no windows, so the representatives don't hear noise from outside. Members meet in the House Chamber to talk about bills that may become laws.

Representatives have offices near the Capitol in Washington, D.C. They work in their offices when they are not in the House Chamber.

The Longworth House building holds offices for representatives.

A representative works at a desk in an office. But he may also work in many other places.

They go to meetings. They make phone calls. They read mail from people in their state. Representatives work in their home states too.

Did You Know?

John Dingell Jr. worked for the House for the longest amount of time. He was a representative from Michigan for 59 years!

Alexandria Ocasio-Cortez is the youngest woman to become a member of the House. She was 29 years old when she became the representative for New York's 14th district.

There have been 19 representatives from the House that have been elected president of the United States.

Fast Facts

- The House of Representatives is part of the U.S. government.

- There are 435 members in the House of Representatives.

- The House of Representatives sees every bill before it becomes a law.

- Representatives from every state are elected every two years.

Glossary

bill (BIL)—a plan for a new law

candidate (KAN-duh-dayt)—a person who wants a job in government

committee (kuh-MI-tee)—a group of people chosen to discuss things and make decisions for a larger group

Congress (KAHNG-gruhs)—the elected government body of the United States that makes laws; Congress includes the Senate and the House of Representatives.

election (i-LEK-shuhn)—the act of choosing people to work in government

government (GUHV-urn-muhnt)—the group of people who make laws, rules, and decisions for a country or state

law (LAW)—a rule made by the government that must be obeyed

legislative branch (LEJ-iss-lay-tiv BRANCH)—one of the three parts of the U.S. government; this part makes rules and laws for people to follow

Senate (SEN-it)—one of the two houses of the U.S. Congress that makes laws

term (TERM)—a set amount of time for a job

veto (VEE-toh)—the power or right to stop a bill from becoming law

vote (VOHT)—a choice made by a person based on their own views

Read More

Ferguson, Melissa. *U.S. Government: What You Need to Know.* North Mankato, MN: Capstone Press, 2017.

McAuliffe, Bill. *The U.S. House of Representatives.* Mankato, MN: Creative Education, 2016.

Rose, Simon. *House of Representatives.* New York: SmartBook Media Inc., 2018.

Internet Sites

Kids in the House: What is Congress?
https://kids-clerk.house.gov/grade-school/lesson.html?intID=1

10 Facts About the House of Representatives
https://www.borgenmagazine.com/10-facts-about-the-house-of-representatives/

Index